SCOTT RUBIN

THE ESSENTIAL GUIDE TO

MY NEW LIFE
WITH JESUS

simply for students

The Essential Guide to My New Life With Jesus
© 2016 Scott Rubin

group.com
simplyyouthministry.com

Credits
Author: Scott Rubin
Executive Developer: Tim Gilmour
Executive Editor: Rick Lawrence
Chief Creative Officer: Joani Schultz
Editor: Stephanie Martin
Art Director and Cover Art: Veronica Preston
Production: Veronica Preston
Project Manager: Justin Boling

Unless otherwise indicated, all Scripture quotations are taken from the New Living Translation, copyright © 1996, 2004, 2007. Used by permission of Tyndale House Publishers, Inc., Carol Stream, Illinois 60188. All rights reserved.

ISBN 978-1-4707-3613-2
10 9 8 7 6 5 4 3 2 1   21 20 19 18 17 16

Printed in the United States of America.

TABLE OF CONTENTS

INTRODUCTION

That's because it means you've discovered the greatest gift ever: the fact that Jesus is crazy about you and wants to give you the fullest kind of life imaginable. Whatever your life has been like up to this point, intentionally inviting Jesus into it changes everything! I realize people often use the term "life-changing" for things that really aren't, but in this case it's so true.

This is personal for me because I remember becoming a Christian at age 17. Oh sure, I knew "of" Jesus before then and had heard some general stuff about him. But it honestly didn't seem to have much to do with my life.

So when somebody invited me to a summer camp where they'd be talking about Jesus, I hesitated. But this camp had waterskiing, parasailing, and a sweet beach. Plus, a bunch of my buddies were going, as well as a few cute girls. With all that awesomeness, I figured I could put up with a little "God talk" at camp. How bad could it be?

One night that week, though, someone clearly explained what it meant to be a Christian. Not only did it make sense, it blew my mind. I realized that knowing about Jesus wasn't enough. I recognized that his death on the cross was a game-changer for me personally.

And I figured out that faith demanded a commitment from me. Did I believe in Jesus as God's Son or not? Would I invite him to lead my life or not?

That summer, I understood a bunch of things in a whole new way. When I decided to follow Jesus, it was the start of an amazing relationship.

I also quickly discovered I didn't understand a bunch of stuff about following Jesus. Certain Christian "codes" were a mystery. No one in the church was intentionally keeping secrets from me, but sometimes I felt as if I'd missed the first week of a new school year; everybody else at church seemed to know stuff I didn't.

This book will clue you in on some of that stuff. If you've ever been the "new kid" in any situation, you know how much it helps to have someone show you around. I hope these chapters give you a tour of the awesomeness of following Jesus!

Read the book from start to finish or a little bit at a time. You can also jump around to different sections that look interesting— whatever helps you most.

One last thought: Although this book will answer some of your questions, it might also raise more. Think of a Christian you know, and ask him or her any questions that come up as you read. If someone gave you this book, he or she will probably be honored to serve as a resource.

READY? LET'S DO THIS!

SECTION 1:

CONGRATS!

CAUSE FOR A PARTY

Imagine what a party would look like if Jesus were hosting it. Now imagine it's not at someone's house or even a fancy restaurant but actually in heaven.

Believing in Jesus and beginning your life with him is the biggest step a person can make. And the Bible says it sets off a huge celebratory bash among the angels—all for one individual.

CHECK OUT THIS BIBLE VERSE:

"In the same way, there is more joy in heaven over one lost sinner who repents and returns to God than over ninety-nine others who are righteous and haven't strayed away!"

Luke 15:7

When I first understood what Jesus did for me, I figured it was a big deal but definitely didn't grasp that following him was party-worthy. Why the big deal? Because Jesus loves you more than you can imagine. And he created you with the hope that you'd recognize him and invite him into your heart and life.

Jesus won't force his way into your life, though; that's not his style. So when you ask him to show you the best way to live, he's ready to do just that. Jesus knows what a difference it will make—both for you and for the people you impact.

As I type these words, my heart is beating faster and my knee is bouncing uncontrollably—and it's not because I've had too much caffeine. It's because I'm excited for you, knowing that your adventure with Jesus is underway.

Like the angels, I'm partying, too—about you and what's ahead for your relationship with Jesus.

RELATIONSHIP, NOT RELIGION

What does Jesus want most from us? That question often trips people up.

A popular but incorrect answer is that Jesus mainly wants us to behave well. They think he's looking for people who will be good, color inside the lines, and get "good behavior" stamped on their report cards.

People who buy into that good-behavior myth focus on two areas: the Don'ts and the Shoulds. The Don'ts are bad stuff not to do. You know that circle with the line through it? Some people see it all over the place when they think about Jesus and the Bible:

◊ **Don't lie. Don't cheat. Don't cuss.**
◊ **Don't do mean stuff.**
◊ **Don't drink or do drugs or anything illegal.**
◊ **Don't have sex.**

PLEASE DO NOT SET YOURSELF ON FIRE

THANK YOU FOR YOUR COOPERATION

DO NOT TOUCH! NOT ONLY WILL THIS KILL YOU

DANGER

IT WILL HURT THE WHOLE TIME YOU ARE DYING

The second area, the Shoulds, is good stuff to work harder at. It's like a holy to-do list:

◊ **Read your Bible.**
◊ **Pray more. (How much is "enough"? Who knows. Probably more than I'm doing.)**
◊ **Be polite. (Do good deeds, hold doors, help old ladies across streets.)**

Yes, of course your life looks different after you start following Jesus. But ultimately, he isn't after the Don'ts and the Shoulds. More than anything else, you know what Jesus really wants? He wants to be with you! That's true on your best days and your worst. It's true when you're a candidate for Student of the Month and a candidate for detention.

In the Bible, a guy named Jacob followed God but did some bad stuff. (You can read about it in Genesis 27.) Jacob cheated his brother big-time—enough that he feared for his life and left town. But then God sent a sign to remind Jacob that he was still with him. And Jacob ended up saying,

"Surely the Lord is in this place, and I wasn't even aware of it!"

Genesis 28:16

That's the cool thing about Jesus: He never leaves you, even when your behavior doesn't look very Christian.

SO REMEMBER:

Jesus wants more than your good behavior; he wants to be with you and have a relationship with you.

SECTION 2:

OPENING TIPS

SHARE YOUR NEWS

Part of the fun of having great news is getting to share it with somebody. When your team wins, it's way more fun celebrating with teammates than being happy alone. When school's closed because of a blizzard, kids text one another to share the joyous news. But absolutely nothing is cooler than when someone truly understands Jesus' love for them. So undoubtedly that's news worth sharing!

If you need a little more convincing, here are three reasons you shouldn't keep quiet about your new or growing relationship with Jesus:

1.   SHARING THE THRILL.

Other people who follow Jesus will be totally excited to hear what you've discovered. It's even better than when a friend discovers one of your favorite songs or restaurants.

2.   SHARING THE TEAMWORK.

One of the best parts of the Christian adventure is how Jesus equips you to make a difference in the world. Having partners in that ministry provides momentum and multiplies the buzz.

3.   SHARING THE TESTS.

Following Jesus isn't always easy, and you'll face challenges along the way. When fellow Christians are available to help you over the hurdles, though, that makes a huge difference.

You might be tempted to think, "Nah, faith is just a private thing for me. I'm not sure anyone would really care that much, anyway." Please reconsider! Christianity involves teamwork and support, so the more people you're linked up with, the better.

Now for the key question: **Who should you tell about your relationship with Jesus?** Basically, anyone you haven't told yet. Anyone who'd be stoked to share in the celebration.

Think of one person you can talk to about this in the next 24 hours, and write his or her name in this box:

Now plan to call, text, or meet in person and say,

"I'm a Christian, I'm going to follow Jesus, and I really wanted to tell you!"

Believe me, that person will be even happier than hearing about a snow day!

NO PERFECT CHRISTIANS

Imagine getting all the answers right on every test you took. Or scoring on every shot you made in basketball or soccer or lacrosse. Unreasonable, right? Perfection just doesn't exist for humans.

Yet when it comes to following Jesus, sometimes we feel as if we shouldn't make any mistakes. Don't fall into that trap! We simply won't "get it right" all the time.

But doesn't Jesus want us to stay away from sin? Definitely true. He knows, though, that humans don't hit the bull's-eye every time, so he planned ahead for that.

John, a follower of Jesus, explained it this way in the Bible:

"My dear children, I am writing this to you so that you will not sin. But if anyone does sin, we have an advocate who pleads our case before the Father. He is Jesus Christ, the one who is truly righteous." **1 John 2:1**

You have an advocate, the Bible says. What exactly is that? Simply, it's someone who pleads your case and supports you. Jesus, who is God and is with God, constantly reminds his Father of the price he's already paid for you. "I know that person," Jesus says. "They're with me, and I've covered them."

When I was a kid, I often got blamed for stuff. Even though I had three siblings, when something was broken or missing or messed up, usually the finger was pointed at me. (Truth is, I often was to blame…but not always!)

But then Grandma Hoover came to visit. She really liked me and often pleaded my case before my mom: "Scott did do that, but he's a good boy. I love him." Sometimes that got me off the hook.

It's similar—but even better—with Jesus. He knows you aren't perfect, but he's right next to God the Father, reminding him that you belong to him, even when you make mistakes.

So if someone says you need to be perfect to be a Christian, confidently assure them, "That's not how it works!" Then share who's advocating on your behalf—and theirs.

MORE THAN A FEELING

The few first days after I became a Christian, I felt so different. It wasn't as if all my problems or worries had disappeared; I just had a confidence from knowing I wasn't alone.

Jesus was with me and offering me his strength.

My faith journey began with a fantastic week at camp. I was surrounded by great friends—some new and some old. I was away from all the "normal-ness" of regular life, having a blast and thinking about Jesus in a new way. As I rode the bus home, I remember wishing I could stay at camp a few more days because regular life probably wouldn't feel as shiny.

In the Bible, three of Jesus' followers (or disciples) had a similar experience, but way more intense. You can read it at the beginning of Matthew 17. Jesus took Peter, James, and John to a mountaintop, and they heard God speaking from the sky. Two other important people from the Bible (Moses and Elijah) showed up, too.

The experience rocked Jesus' followers so much they didn't want to leave. Peter came up with a great idea (or so he thought) and suggested it to Jesus: "Let's build some shelters up here and just stay!" In other words, Peter wanted to capture the feeling of that moment and make it last.

But Jesus knew that mountaintop living isn't what the world needs. Christians can't hide away from the world's problems, challenges, and junk. When we meet Jesus and commit to following him, we need to head down the mountain and bring Jesus' light to people who haven't been up there.

On your journey with Jesus, remember that he's way more than a feeling. Jesus is a constant companion, ready to walk with you into any hills and valleys you face.

? HOW CAN I BE SURE I'M A CHRISTIAN?

Someone might have handed you this book after you met Jesus. Or maybe you picked it up on your own, to learn more about honoring Jesus with your life. No matter where you are in your walk with Jesus, I wouldn't be surprised if you occasionally wondered:

"Am I really a Christian? How can I be sure?"

You see, I really mess up sometimes. I wouldn't say some of my thoughts out loud to Jesus, for example. Meanwhile, the really good Christians seem to be honoring Jesus way more than I am.

A two-word phrase in that last sentence is confusing and simply false: good Christians.

A common misunderstanding is that God has a giant scale, weighs the good stuff we've done, compares it to the bad stuff we've done, and determines if we're somehow "in." Nope, that's not how Christianity works, thankfully.

Paul, who called himself the worst of sinners because he used to kill Jesus' followers before becoming one, wrote many letters that became part of the Bible.

In Ephesians 2:8-9, he said:

> God saved you by his grace when you believed. And you can't take credit for this; it is a gift from God. Salvation is not a reward for the good things we have done, so none of us can boast about it.

Did you catch that? Being a Christian is about what you believe, not about what you do!

Faith isn't about how you can earn God's favor; instead, it's about what Jesus already did for each of us by dying on the cross.

To be clear, here's how you can be sure you're a Christian:

Do you believe that Jesus, God's Son, came to live on earth?

Do you believe he lived a perfect life…and you haven't?

Do you believe that Jesus died and rose again to pay for your imperfection?

And do you want Jesus to lead your life?

Then guess what?

You're a Christian…and that can't be taken away.

THE ESSENTIAL GUIDE TO

MY NEW LIFE WITH JESUS

SECTION 3:

READ

THIS SECTION HAS ONE PURPOSE:

TO CONVINCE YOU THAT THE BIBLE IS AMAZING.

You may not consider yourself a reader, or you may have tons of questions about the Bible. But this incredible resource contains life guidance directly from God.

Let me share an analogy (I heard some of these things from a pastor named Andy Stanley):

Some people have a natural sense of direction, and others… just don't. If you headed outside right now, what's the farthest place you could go without getting lost? What if you had to direct someone to the nearest big city, without referring to Google Maps? Some people might know exactly where to turn, while others…well, you'd probably have to send out a search party.

Signs give travelers directions, but they're useless if you can't tell what they're saying.

Check out these less-than-helpful signs, posted at the Travel Channel website:

The Bible, also called God's Word or Holy Scripture, is like a road sign for life. God gave us the Bible as a source of direction. The Bible has helped me countless times, guiding me to much better thoughts, plans, and ideas than I would've come up with on my own.

The Bible is the most important book on the planet, yet it's way more than that. And actually, it's not even a book! (Stick with me here.) It's a collection of 66 historical documents, called books, written by 40 different authors throughout many centuries. They all point to God's loving plan to send Jesus to save us.

Let's look at what the Bible says about its purpose:

> All Scripture is inspired by God and is useful to teach us what is true and to make us realize what is wrong in our lives. It corrects us when we are wrong and teaches us to do what is right. God uses it to prepare and equip his people to do every good work.
>
> **2 Timothy 3:16-17**

Did you catch that?

Jesus wants you to know what's in the Bible so he can help you live for him!

Extra credit: Grab a Bible, read 2 Timothy 3:16-17 again, and ask Jesus to help you grow through reading Scripture.

UNDERSTANDING IS KEY

Now that you're energized about reading the Bible so Jesus can speak to you, it's essential to understand what that written Word is saying.

When I was in sixth grade, my grandma gave me my first Bible—one of hers. She looked ancient, but that Bible seemed even older. It looked like something you'd find in an antique bookstore. I tried to read it (after the moths flew out) but never got very far. Deciphering the big, unfamiliar words was a major chore.

When you were younger, maybe you had a children's Bible with colorful pictures and smiling cartoon faces. It wasn't an actual Bible but gave you the idea of the contents. That's fine for little kids, but now you need a Bible that challenges your smarter brain.

The Bible is the best-selling book in history; about 5 billion copies have been printed.

But you may have noticed different

versions, or translations, of the Bible.

What does that mean?

Although we may imagine Jesus speaking English when he walked the earth, he actually spoke Aramaic (pronounced *Air-uh-**may**-ick*). Some of the New Testament's first books were written in that language, while others were in Hebrew and Greek.

Throughout the years, scholars translated the Bible into different languages. But even in English, more than 100 Bible versions exist. That's because different authors interpreted certain words and phrases differently. For example, the King James Version (KJV) from the early 1600s would be a great Bible if you spoke the way people spoke then, with words such as "thee," "thyself," "loveth," and "believeth."

Here's 2 Corinthians 6:2 in the KJV:

For he saith, I have heard thee in a time accepted, and in the day of salvation have I succoured thee: behold, now is the accepted time; behold, now is the day of salvation.

Here's the same verse from the modern-day New Living Translation (NLT):

For God says, "At just the right time, I heard you. On the day of salvation, I helped you." Indeed, the "right time" is now. Today is the day of salvation.

The difference is pretty obvious, don't you thinketh?

As language changes, translators continue creating updated Bible versions, so it comes down to which one you understand best. Many students prefer the NLT or NIV (New International Version). When you're selecting a Bible, take time to read some verses and see if the wording is clear. Also ask the advice of a Christian you trust.

Bonus note: Besides different versions, some Bibles include various notes and comments. For example, you'll see study Bibles, one-year Bibles, men's Bibles, women's Bibles, etc.—all of which can be helpful. But the version (or translation) is most important.

HOW TO FIND
BIBLE VERSES

I love inside jokes—when I'm on the inside, that is. It's fun when friends have known each other long enough that they crack up at the mention of a single word. What I don't love is being on the outside when somebody else uses insider language. That's just awkward.

Some aspects of church can make you feel as if you're on the outside. A big one is how to look up Bible verses.

As I mentioned earlier, the Bible is a historical document consisting of 66 books. The Old Testament has 39, and the New Testament has 27. (The first four books of the New Testament—Matthew, Mark, Luke, and John—tell about Jesus' life, death, and resurrection. They're known as the Gospels, which means "good news.")

Each book of the Bible is divided into chapters, similar to other books you read. But then each chapter is broken down even further, into verses. When you read the Bible and see tiny numbers in the middle of paragraphs, those are verses.

Often a verse is just a sentence long. But it can be more than one sentence or even just a couple of words. (The Bible wasn't originally divided into verses; people added them throughout history—probably because they got tired of saying, "It's about two-thirds of the way through the chapter…halfway down the page.")

So here's the "insider language": When people talk about a Bible verse, they usually say it as the book, then the chapter, then the verse. So, for example, James 4:8 is in the book of James, chapter 4, verse 8.

BOOK → **CHAPTER** → **VERSE**

A Bible's table of contents lists all the books in order, along with page numbers for easy reference. Many Bibles also have a helpful resource called an index or concordance in the back so you can find verses about certain topics. For example, to locate all the places where the Bible talks about peace, find the word "peace" in the concordance, and you'll see a list of all the verses that use it.

The best way to familiarize yourself with your Bible and how to find verses is…to read it. **As you dive in, you'll become more comfortable with the format and also learn more about Jesus' never-ending love for you.** Plus, you'll notice Jesus speaking directly to you, about your own life. And that's the best insider language I can think of.

WHAT IS "MEDITATING" ON SCRIPTURE?

That's a puzzling phrase for many young people—and even adults. Sometimes I'm asked, "Isn't meditation a creepy thing that fortune tellers do on *Scooby-Doo?*"

I love questions about faith. How can we understand if we don't ask?

Remember, Scripture is what's written in the Bible. So meditating on Scripture simply means thinking deeply or focusing on part of the Bible. That's important because Jesus wants the Bible to do more than just *inform* you; he wants it to *transform* you.

Here are three keys to experiencing the Bible's power in your life:

1. UNDERSTAND IT.

If you have questions, ask! I still wonder about stuff and learn new things when I read the Bible, and I'm old.

2. UNDERLINE IT.

Just because the Bible is a holy book doesn't mean you can't write in it. In fact, underlining interesting things you read makes them jump out at you later. Get braver and write notes in the margins, which is a great way to interact with God's Word.

3. "WEAR" IT.

Or, to keep the theme from the other two points, "(under) Wear It." (Hey, whatever helps you remember!) What does wearing the Bible mean? You actually have to try it on. If you just read and underline, you'll miss the key point: You need to decide to live out the Bible's message, walk around in it, wear it.

James 4:8, a Bible verse I've always liked, says:

Come close to God, and God will come close to you.

To "wear" those words this week meant I chose to pull closer to God during a challenging conversation, when I was sad about a family member's illness, and as I watched a gorgeous sunset. And you know what? **Living out that Bible verse changed how I experienced those different situations and emotions. I felt closer to Jesus and not alone.**

You can meditate on Scripture almost anywhere—during some quiet reading time, in between classes, or while interacting with your family. Plus, you can start memorizing the verse you're focusing on.

Being able to recall certain Bible verses is like having a supply of Jesus' wisdom, hope, and direction always at your fingertips, helping you navigate life with him.

Understand the Bible, underline it, and (under)wear it. And get underway today!

WHAT IF I DON'T UNDERSTAND SOMETHING?

Even when you use a Bible with clear language and an appropriate reading level, you still might hit some bumps in the road. You may recognize the words themselves but not grasp the concept Jesus is trying to tell you.

First off, you aren't alone.

Hundreds of scholars throughout the centuries have researched, studied, and debated the meaning of various Scripture passages. Yet they still have different opinions about the significance or implication. Some parts of the Bible are tied to the customs and culture of when the words were written, so we can't fully relate.

Maybe a section's meaning is related to a next-step spiritual truth you'll need to talk through with a Christian adult. Other times, it's a concept Jesus will have to explain to us in heaven someday; for now, we can only try to live out what we think it means.

First Corinthians 13:12 says:

Now we see things imperfectly, like puzzling reflections in a mirror, but then we will see everything with perfect clarity. All that I know now is partial and incomplete, but then I will know everything completely, just as God now knows me completely.

That verse reminds me that until I go to heaven, I won't fully understand some things about Jesus and the Bible. But it also assures me that he knows me completely and will provide everything I need to live the way he asks me to live.

So keep reading the Bible, even when certain parts don't make total sense. Jesus will keep using his words to strengthen you as you follow him.

Whatever you do, though, don't fake it. People who claim to understand everything in the Bible—even if they're pastors or college professors—aren't being truthful. So don't feel uncomfortable admitting when you don't know an answer. Saying "I don't know" is okay.

In fact, being honest about what you don't understand—and continuing to search—can be what leads you to the answer.

WHAT IF I DON'T FEEL LIKE READING THE BIBLE?

That's a great, honest question—one that deserves an honest answer.

Have you ever been on a sports team and just didn't want to go to a workout? Or maybe you love music and are supposed to practice 30 minutes every day but just don't feel like it.

We've all been there. Sure, we know Jesus uses the Bible to communicate with us and help us experience his power, the same way we know practicing the tuba leads to being a better tuba player. But even longtime Christians can struggle with wanting to read the Bible.

Whenever I sit down to read Scripture but really don't feel like it, I spend a minute or two thinking about Jesus before even opening the book. I think about specific ways he's blessed and supported me. **I remember that the Bible is Jesus' tool to help me live differently.** And sometimes I flat-out pray that he'll help me want to read his Word.

Sometimes when I finish those thoughts, I can't wait to open my Bible and see what Jesus wants to show me. Other times, reading still admittedly feels like a chore, so I read it out of obedience. And maybe nothing jumps off the page at me, so I close my Bible and go on with my day.

Here's a verse I've been "meditating" on that's related to this:

> No discipline is enjoyable while it is happening—it's painful! But afterward there will be a peaceful harvest of right living for those who are trained in this way. **Hebrews 12:11**

When I obey Jesus, sometimes he surprises me. I'll go through my day, interacting with people, and a thought pops into my head that I wouldn't have had on my own. Then I remember encountering it in the Bible, even when I hadn't felt like reading.

Jesus brought the thought to my mind and provided a way to apply it to my life.

Experiencing Jesus that way is powerful. Even better than playing the tuba.

SECTION 4:

PRAY

24/7 ACCESS

You've probably had a conversation with Siri, the iPhone voice that answers questions, gives directions, and even has a sense of humor. Like Siri, Jesus is always "on call," and he's a trustworthy source of truth and answers.

But that's where the similarities end. Unlike Siri, Jesus listens to your feelings, thoughts, confusion—everything. He's there 24/7, with perfect reception and no battery that needs recharging.

Jesus hears you every time, all the time, any time. Best of all, he's the ultimate source of wisdom.

If you ever question whether Jesus is listening to you, read Psalm 34:

I prayed to the LORD, and he answered me. He freed me from all my fears. **(verse 4)**

In my desperation I prayed, and the LORD listened; he saved me from all my troubles. **(verse 6)**

The eyes of the LORD watch over those who do right; his ears are open to their cries for help. **(verse 15)**

The LORD hears his people when they call to him for help. He rescues them from all their troubles. **(verse 17)**

All of that's in just one chapter of the Bible! Throughout Scripture, Jesus promises to listen any time we want or need to talk to him.*

Think about that: **The Creator of the universe, the King of everything, is available to you 24/7.** That makes me want to pray even more, about everything.

*More verses to explore:

Then if my people who are called by my name will humble themselves and pray and seek my face and turn from their wicked ways, I will hear from heaven and will forgive their sins and restore their land. My eyes will be open and my ears attentive to every prayer made in this place (2 Chronicles 7:14-15).

O people of Zion, who live in Jerusalem, you will weep no more. He will be gracious if you ask for help. He will surely respond to the sound of your cries (Isaiah 30:19).

And we are confident that he hears us whenever we ask for anything that pleases him. And since we know he hears us when we make our requests, we also know that he will give us what we ask for (1 John 5:14-15).

"PRETTY PRAYERS" NOT REQUIRED

Ever hear of a life hack? It's a shortcut or new idea that makes a task or process easier.

Here are a few. (I'm not saying they're brilliant. You decide.)

LIFE HACKS
THAT YOU MAY OR MAY NOT HAVE KNOWN

MAKE A PLAYLIST FOR THE AMOUNT OF TIME YOU HAVE TO GET READY IN THE MORNING. YOU'LL HAVE A "MUSICAL" REMINDER OF HOW MUCH TIME YOU HAVE LEFT.

ICE-COLD DRINK IN 3 MINUTES IN A POT, ADD A SODA CAN, COVER WITH ICE, AND ADD 2 CUPS OF SALT. FILL WITH WATER. WAIT 3 MINUTES.

THE BEST BACON RUN BACON UNDER COLD WATER BEFORE BAKING AT 365 DEGREES FOR 10 MINUTES. THE WATER PREVENTS IT FROM SHRINKING.

START A FIRE WITH NO KINDLING DORITOS WORK AS A PERFECT FIRE-STARTER, IF YOU DON'T HAVE TRADITIONAL WOOD CHIPS OR KINDLING.

I used to wish I had a life hack for knowing how to talk to Jesus. After all, prayer can feel kind of intimidating: What's okay to say and what isn't? What's the right way to ask questions? What do I need to remember to thank Jesus for?

So I came up with a life hack for prayer…but I skipped the "k," so it's actually a life hac. The simple acronym helps you remember that talking to Jesus doesn't have to sound or look a certain way. It's more about your heart.

Each letter represents a word that's important to prayer:

H   HONOR

Tell Jesus something you think is cool about him.

A   ASK

Share your requests.

C   CONFESS

Admit where you've messed up and need Jesus' forgiveness.

Thinking about all three areas is important because it's easy to get consumed by what we need (or want). Or we might forget to give Jesus honor and to confess our sins. "Honor, Ask, Confess" can help you pray more completely and focus on Jesus, not just yourself.

When you don't know what to pray, write those three letters down the side of a paper and then write a sentence or two to Jesus. You can even read it out loud as a reminder that he's really hearing it.

PRAYER IS THAT SIMPLE.

Jesus isn't looking for long, compound-complex sentences with big, pretty words. He truly wants to know your heart—what you're thankful for, what you're concerned about, and how you've gotten off track. He wants to hear it all...exactly the way you want to share it.

PRAYING BACKWARDS?

Usually when you do something backwards, you get different results. My sons managed to put their shirts on backwards a lot when they were little, which made mornings more hectic. Soon after getting my license, I tried driving backwards and rammed into a street light. I've thrown a bowling ball down the lane backwards, but the results weren't much different from when I bowl forwards.

What does that have to do with praying? A book called *Praying Backwards* by Bryan Chapell really helped me think about how to talk to Jesus. People can get overly concerned with what words to use and in what order—you know, how to talk "appropriately" to Jesus. Some people think they need to start their prayers with holy-sounding words and finish with "In Jesus' name, amen."

That phrase is fine, but if you're not careful, "In Jesus' name" can become mindless. I've ended a prayer that way when the prayer wasn't something Jesus would want at all.

Praying backwards means starting prayers with what Jesus wants instead of what you want. The goal of prayer should be about getting on the same page as Jesus, rather than trying to get him on the same page as you.

Jesus cares more about your attitude and heart than the specific words you use.

Check out what Jesus says in Matthew 6:7-10:

"When you pray, don't babble on and on as people of other religions do. They think their prayers are answered merely by repeating their words again and again. Don't be like them, for your Father knows exactly what you need even before you ask him! Pray like this: Our Father in heaven, may your name be kept holy. May your kingdom come soon. May your will be done on earth, as it is in heaven."

In these verses, Jesus decides he wants to care first about what God cares about. That's not always how we pray. Often we start by listing everything we think we need. Sometimes we pray, "God, can my will be done, here on earth? Here's my will: I want to win this game, get a good grade, be treated differently. Does that work out okay for you? Thanks! Peace out! In Jesus' name, amen."

Yes, Jesus tells us to let him know what we want:

"You can ask for anything in my name, and I will do it, so that the Son can bring glory to the Father. Yes, ask me for anything in my name, and I will do it!" (John 14:13-14).

But if we model our prayers after Jesus' prayer (also called the Lord's Prayer), we'll start in a different place. **Our attitude— our heart—will focus on God first.**

I want to challenge you to pray backwards this week. As a reminder, pick something you're wearing or something in your bedroom, and turn it backwards. Whenever you see that, remember to put Jesus' will ahead of your own when you pray!

TALKING *AND* LISTENING

I almost missed one of the best opportunities in my life: my job as a youth pastor. I was working at church, helping newly married couples, and a church leader called. He asked me to consider being the middle school pastor. My first thought? "Nah, I'm good. I'm pretty sure Jesus isn't asking me to do that." But that didn't sound very spiritual, so instead I replied, "I'll pray about it." So, I actually did pray about it, and here I am—a middle school pastor.

When you pray, how can you really listen so you hear from Jesus? Well, it probably won't happen by accident or when your focus is on something else. You probably won't hear from Jesus while you're playing games on the iPad, taking notes in class, or hanging out at the movies.

This Bible verse is one of my all-time favorites:

"The eyes of the LORD search the whole earth in order to strengthen those whose hearts are fully committed to him."

2 Chronicles 16:9

Wow—God is looking to see if we're looking for him!
He's searching to see if we're committed to him and ready
to do what he asks.

Like me, you may be motivated to listen to God but unsure
how to start. There's no secret formula, but these tips really
help:

1. FIND A SPACE.

That sounds simple enough, but some people never do it.
Pick a spot to go to regularly when you want to listen to
Jesus. You'll get used to hanging out with him there, which
will help you get in a listening mindset.

2. INVITE JESUS TO HANG OUT.

Really. Start by saying this out loud: "Jesus, here I am. I
want to talk with you, and I invite you to talk with me. I'm
listening."

3. READ SOME BIBLE VERSES...

...to start thinking about God. Opening up God's Word will help you focus on him.

4. ASK JESUS...

...if he has anything he wants to say to you. Then quietly listen. Remember, the God of the universe has promised to offer guidance and wisdom. His voice is more like a gentle whisper than a loud shout, though, and you need to be patient. You might not hear anything instantly, but you may eventually sense Jesus reminding you of something ("I'm nearby," "I love you like crazy") or directing you to do something (encourage a friend, apologize for saying something, serve your family).

5. DO SOMETHING ABOUT IT!

Once you get an idea of what Jesus is asking you to do, be courageous and follow through on it. If you're willing to obey do what God tells you, you'll likely hear from him more and more.

IS PRAYER REALLY NECESSARY?

Certainly I'm not the only person who's wondered: **"If Jesus already knows everything, what's the point of praying?"**

Have you ever been hanging out with a good buddy who totally surprised you with his or her thoughts? Maybe you were talking about YouTube videos and your friend liked one you never would've expected. Or maybe you were discussing a teacher you don't like and discovered your friend thought that person is one of the school's best. Even in our closest relationships, we can be surprised by someone else's thoughts or insights.

In John 15:15, Jesus calls us his friends, and praying to him is like growing that friendship (not only about asking for things).

Because Jesus knows everything, the focus of prayer isn't to inform him about what's new with you. Instead, it's more about inviting him into every part of your life—the ups and downs, the questions and wonderings.

When you spend consistent time with Jesus, the things you want will begin to line up with the things he wants for you. As a kid, I once asked God to make me the smartest person in the world. (Don't judge me. I was young!) Why did I want that? For selfish reasons, of course.

James 4:3 says:

> And even when you ask, you don't get it because your motives are all wrong—you want only what will give you pleasure.

When you grow your relationship with Jesus through prayer, he'll help you think about your intentions and align them with his plan for you.

Finally, telling Jesus what's on your heart expresses your dependence on him and gives him space to grow you. Over time, Jesus will shape your character by helping you become more patient, loving, joyful, peaceful, kind, generous, faithful, good, gentle, and self-controlled. But that happens only when you maintain a consistent, prayerful relationship with him.

QUANTITY AND QUALITY

If you love summer as much as I do, then the first day of school is especially tough. Not only does it mark the end of warm, outside days, but teachers spend that first class reviewing the rules and expectations and explaining how to get a good grade. How will you measure up against your new classmates?

That brings up another great thing about prayer: There's no grading scale! Jesus doesn't judge your prayers or compare them to other people's prayers. He never says: "That's a C+ prayer. You can do better than that."

The Bible does, however, contain valuable information about how to pray:

"Rejoice in our confident hope. Be patient in trouble, and keep on praying."

(Romans 12:12)

"Pray in the Spirit at all times and on every occasion. Stay alert and be persistent in your prayers for all believers everywhere." **(Ephesians 6:18)**

"Don't worry about anything; instead, pray about everything. Tell God what you need, and thank him for all he has done." **(Philippians 4:6)**

"Devote yourselves to prayer with an alert mind and a thankful heart." **(Colossians 4:2)**

Although Jesus doesn't grade your prayers, he wants to be part of your life as much as you'll let him. And prayer is a great way for that to happen.

Prayer is such a vital part of following Jesus, and it can happen throughout your day. When you're bummed out, or feeling grateful, or stressed about what the future holds, tell Jesus and ask for his guidance.

You can pray a sentence or two to Jesus any time, in any place. Nothing is too big for him to handle or too small for him to care about, and he's always listening.

Can you think of a one-sentence prayer for Jesus right now? Pray it—knowing you won't be graded!

WHAT IF JESUS DOESN'T ANSWER?

I don't like trick questions, but this title is a trick question. **The truth is that Jesus does answer our prayers—every single one.** But sometimes it's not how we expect. Other times it's in a way that doesn't make sense to us at the time.

Remember when you were little and begged for candy, and your mom or dad said no? That wasn't what you wanted to hear. At other times, your requests received a "yes" or "not yet."

Jesus isn't a holy vending machine where you make a request, push a button, and—ta da!—get what you want. Jesus does hear every request, but because he can see a bigger picture than we can, he'll answer in the way he knows is best.

In Luke 22:42, Jesus prayed:

"Father, if you are willing, please take this cup of suffering away from me. Yet I want your will to be done, not mine."

Jesus was about to be arrested and then killed. He didn't want to face the suffering and pain ahead. But God the Father didn't give Jesus the answer he wanted to hear at the time. Ultimately, though, God's "no" saved us, because Jesus' death paid for all our sins.

Think about prayers Jesus doesn't answer the way you want. I have the greatest wife, but you know what I prayed for in college? "Jesus, will you please work things out for me with this other girl?" Who knows where I'd be now if he'd answered "yes."

What if you prayed and asked Jesus to allow you to go to a party, but he knew you'd end up getting hurt? Although you'd be upset at the time, ultimately that "no" would be best for you.

Look at Luke 22:42 again, and check out the last sentence. Jesus asked for God's will to be done, not his own. Putting God's will first means getting on the same page with him and lining up your requests with what matters most to him. It means focusing on Jesus' love for you, his death for your sins, and the steps you might need to take to follow him more closely. (Do you need to forgive someone? treat someone differently? do something to help someone else?)

Romans 8:28 says:

And we know that God causes everything to work together for the good of those who love God and are called according to his purpose for them.

Sometimes you may never know why Jesus answered a prayer the way he did, but you can trust his love and his plan.

Jesus is crazy about you and always wants the best for you.

WHY ASK OTHERS TO PRAY FOR ME?

It can be tough to need stuff from other people. That's why asking for prayer can feel like a weakness.

When Pope Francis recently visited the United States, he repeatedly asked people to pray for him. And he's one of the world's most powerful leaders!

Billy Graham, a wise pastor who advised many presidents, said this about asking others to pray for us: "God urges us not only to pray and commit our burdens to him, but to seek out others who will help us carry our burdens by their prayers."

In the Bible, a "burden" refers to the weight of something you're dealing with that's tough, or sad, or makes you anxious or fearful.

Galatians 6:2 says:

Share each other's burdens, and in this way obey the law of Christ.

The direction is clear: Don't carry your problems alone, Jesus says. Instead, ask people to pray for you, and be willing to pray for others.

Sharing something personal with someone else can be tough. Asking for prayer means you may need to be vulnerable about an area that isn't going well. It can be challenging to reveal stuff in your life that isn't awesome. But it's crucial to find another Christian who cares about you enough to pray for you.

Reality check: The Galatians verse doesn't mean you should walk around asking everyone you meet to pray for you. Sometimes it's best to share your prayer needs with only a few people who know you really well and will respect your confidentiality.

But don't let pride or concern about what others will think stop you from sharing a heavy load that's on your mind or heart. **Ask Jesus for wisdom about confiding your prayer requests with others.**

Don't be alone in the tough stuff.

Asking for prayer is a sign of strength, not weakness!

TIME TO 'FESS UP

My 6-year-old son was playing in our basement when I heard a loud crash. When I walked downstairs, he was standing in a pile of broken glass, baseball bat in hand. A broken light fixture hung above his head.

"Dawson, what happened?" I asked.

"I don't know," he said.

"How'd that light get broken?" I asked.

"I don't know," he repeated.

Really? Wouldn't it have been easier to just admit what he did wrong?

Everybody messes up—you, me, even the best person you know. The Bible has a word for this: sin. Sin can involve doing something you aren't supposed to do or not doing something you are supposed to do. Examples include cheating, stealing, speaking hurtful or untrue words, picking on someone, not defending someone, ignoring your responsibilities, surfing off-limit websites, and so on.

From the beginning of creation, people have tried to deal with sin in various ways:

We rationalize it.

That's a fancy way of saying we explain why a sin isn't a big deal. For example, "That test was way too hard. The teacher couldn't possibly have expected us to memorize all that stuff. Besides, I had a really busy week and no time to study."

We compare it.

We tell ourselves what we did isn't as bad as what so-and-so did. "Sure, I gossiped about that person, but I have a friend who talks trash about people constantly!" Or "I stole just one little thing. This kid I know shoplifts all the time!"

We hide it.

We quickly realize we made a mistake but then think, "If I can somehow hide it, it'll be like it never happened."

Of those three, which have you done? Maybe you've used those sin strategies without even realizing it. **Sin is still sin, though, and it always separates us from Jesus. But thankfully he's already provided a way out.**

First John 1:8-9 says:

If we claim we have no sin, we are only fooling ourselves and not living in the truth. But if we confess our sins to him, he is faithful and just to forgive us our sins and to cleanse us from all wickedness.

When we confess, what does God do with all our sins? Micah 7:19 says he tramples them under his feet and throws them "into the depths of the ocean"!

The deepest part of the ocean, the Mariana Trench, is almost seven miles deep. You could throw Mount Everest in there, and it would be totally covered up. It's so deep, the water pressure would crush a submarine. **God is telling us he completely obliterates our sins when we confess them to him.**

MARIANA TRENCH

Before you turn the page, do you need to confess anything to Jesus?

Don't be afraid to 'fess up. Jesus is waiting to forgive you, and now you know where those sins are heading.

SECTION 5:

TOGETHER

FAITH ISN'T A SOLO SPORT

Whether you're a sports fanatic or don't know a grand slam from a slam dunk, you'll still understand this comparison. Sports fall into two categories: those that are solo in nature, where you depend mainly on yourself, and those that are team-oriented, where you depend on other people. For example, golf is a solo sport, and football is a team sport.

Christians sometimes make the mistake of thinking faith is a solo effort. I know, because it happened to me.

I was beginning my senior year of high school when I truly started understanding who Jesus is. I was learning a lot about him, and some friends were learning along with me. But when I headed to college, I didn't realize the value of finding faith "teammates." I treated my relationship with Jesus as a solo sport, figuring I'd just follow him on my own. And that was way tougher than I'd expected.

In my first weeks of college, I met some great friends. They were fun people, but because they didn't follow Jesus, they were mostly leading themselves. And they didn't always lead themselves into great places.

My new friends started drinking on Friday nights. By the next morning, I was often the only one who remembered anything that had happened.

Let me be clear: My friends weren't bad people. They were just trying to lead themselves...and were getting lost along the way.

One night I left a party and went for a walk by myself. I talked to Jesus out loud, so anyone who saw me might've thought *I'd* been drinking. But that night I started realizing **I needed some fellow teammates who were also training to follow Jesus. We all do!**

EVERYBODY NEEDS A COACH

Let's continue with the sports metaphor. **Not only do you need teammates who can help you follow Jesus, but you'll also benefit from having a coach.** Even the best athletes, musicians, and actors have coaches who encourage them, suggest improvements, and help them eliminate weak spots. LeBron James has a basketball coach, Serena Williams has a tennis coach, and Taylor Swift has a vocal coach. And they're better because of it.

If you're a movie buff, you'll recognize some famous characters who benefitted from a relationship with a mentor-type person. In *Star Wars*, both Luke Skywalker and Anakin were shaped by their relationship with the wise Obi-Wan Kenobi. Uncle Ben counseled Peter Parker (aka Spiderman), while Albus Dumbledore helped Harry Potter and his friends.

Mentors definitely don't need to be perfect. (After all, Haymitch in *The Hunger Games* had a few flaws.) **But what they have in common is they're older, more experienced, and ready to help others travel where they've already been.**

The next question: **What kind of coach should you find?**
Here's some advice:

Look for someone who's "for" you.

Seek a person you trust who really cares about you and wants to see you grow. It might be someone you already know, such as a youth pastor or small-group leader. Maybe it's a relative or older friend.

Look for someone who follows Jesus passionately.

Keep your eyes open for someone who consistently learns more about Jesus and seeks his help. An individual who's growing probably can help you grow, too.

Look for someone who's the same gender as you.

This is a plus, though not a requirement. Someone of your gender can better relate to what you're going through.

One caution: Some people skip the step of finding a coach because they underestimate its importance. Even if your faith journey is going smoothly, you'll probably grow more quickly with a coach. So pray about it and keep looking. If a person or two comes to mind, write their initials here.

TEACHING...BUT NOT LIKE SCHOOL

Have you wondered when you'll ever use some of the facts you're learning in school? In the real world, will you really need to know how long the War of 1812 lasted?

So when you hear it's important to get teaching from church, your first reaction might be, "Hey, I'm not really looking for any more!" But this is a different kind of teaching.

In the Bible, Paul wrote this to Timothy, who was in charge of a young church:

Until I get there, focus on reading the Scriptures to the church, encouraging the believers, and teaching them.

1 Timothy 4:13

That's just one of many places where Scripture instructs churches to teach people—but not with trivial facts that don't relate to your life.

When I tried to learn how to longboard, I was only partially successful. So I got some pointers from a friend, who told me my foot was in the wrong place. Gaining confidence and optimism, one day I decided to tackle a super-steep hill. I picked up so much speed that near the bottom, I got scared and bailed off. But I was going so fast I hit the pavement and rolled. Some nearby construction workers, after realizing I was still alive, just shook their heads.

Later, when I asked my longboard friend if he knew about that hill, he said, "Of course! We call it Idiot Hill…because you'd have to be an idiot to try to go down it."

Good teaching from a church can help you avoid real-life wipeouts. It also can help you know how to patch yourself up if you've already chosen the wrong path.

Do you know of a local youth ministry that offers solid Bible teaching? If you do, attend regularly and listen closely. If you don't, check with a Christian friend or two, and see if they're connected to such a group. **You'll be glad you did!**

WHY YOU NEED OTHER CHRISTIANS— AND THEY NEED YOU

Have you ever used scissors that weren't sharp? They can really rip up a piece of paper. Same thing goes for a knife or ax. Anything that's supposed to be sharp works best when it's really sharp.

To sharpen an ax, you must scrape the blade against something…but not just anything. Scraping it against an apple or your T-shirt won't help. You need something solid.

My dad used to work for a company that made metal grinding wheels that spin around to sharpen things. I brought one to youth group once and sharpened an ax in front of the students, with sparks flying everywhere.

According to the Bible, that kind of sharpening is exactly what happens in friendships:

As iron sharpens iron, so a friend sharpens a friend. **Proverbs 27:17**

Here are three specific ways you and your Jesus-following friends can sharpen one another:

1. A friend goes with you.

To "empathize" means to understand and share someone's feelings. Romans 12:15 says, "Be happy with those who are happy, weep with those who weep." Many people don't do this—only because they don't know what to say. When someone's grandparent dies or their parents divorce, sometimes the only thing you can do is say "I'm sorry" and be sad with that person. You can also share happiness, celebrating when something great happens. Rather than being jealous, a good friend pats your back and says, "That's awesome!"

2. A friend goes second.

You might have a friend who never lets you go first. You mostly do what they want to do and go where they want to go. (On second thought, they might not be a great friend.) Philippians 2:4 says, "Don't look out only for your own interests, but take an interest in others, too." Going second simply means putting another person's needs above your own, no matter the situation. Maybe that means letting your friend choose the movie or have the last Mountain Dew, even though it's the world's greatest drink.

...instead of pulling you away from him. Proverbs 12:26 says, **"The godly give good advice to their friends; the wicked lead them astray."**

Every time I hung out with my friend Aaron, I had a feeling I'd end up in trouble. (Many times, that's exactly what happened.) He was fired up to be the first person to show me pornography. Some friend, huh?

Another friend, Bubba, gave me good advice. Being around him made me feel as if I would make wiser choices—and I did.

So choose your friends well, and make sure you're "sharpening" one another as you follow Jesus.

SECTION 6:

FRIENDS

NO TRADE-INS REQUIRED

What's your favorite type of party? Mine are surprise parties. I love seeing the shocked look on the guest of honor's face when everyone jumps out and yells.

Jesus loved parties because he enjoyed hanging out with all kinds of people. Once Jesus attended a party where tax collectors were on the guest list. In Bible times, tax collectors were hated because they cheated people out of money. Most people avoided them, but not Jesus. (The tax collector named Levi, also known as Matthew, even became one of Jesus' disciples—and wrote a book of the Bible.)

Read what happened at this party:

Later, Levi held a banquet in his home with Jesus as the guest of honor. Many of Levi's fellow tax collectors and other guests also ate with them. But the Pharisees and their teachers of religious law complained bitterly to Jesus' disciples, "Why do you eat and drink with such scum?" Jesus answered them, "Healthy people don't need a doctor— sick people do. I have come to call not those who think they are righteous, but those who know they are sinners and need to repent. **Luke 5:29-32**

The Pharisees and religious teachers, who categorized people as either good or bad, were ticked off. But Jesus wasn't concerned about society's rules. He wants to be around sinful people because he loves them and wants to give them new life.

As you follow Jesus, you don't need to discard your non-Christian friends. **In fact, they need you to live like Jesus— and to point them toward his love for them.** Instead of trading in your old friends, you can add some new Christian friends to your social circles. And your Christian friends can help you show Jesus' love to your non-Christian friends.

Did somebody say *party*?

✝
YOU NEED SOME CHRISTIAN FRIENDS, TOO

You've probably encountered all types of friends, from those who are loyal to those who tear you down. The Bible says:

There are "friends" who destroy each other, but a real friend sticks closer than a brother (Proverbs 18:24).

Friendships also affect your pursuit of wisdom—something the Bible addresses a lot. The book of Proverbs describes the way to have a God-designed life. I love Proverbs because the verses are mostly short, bite-sized gems of truth. It's like reading God-inspired fortune cookies!

Proverbs 11:14 says:

Without wise leadership a nation fails;

there is safety in having many advisers.

In other words, life isn't meant to be tackled alone. Neither is faith. We all need advisers and friends who are pursuing wisdom the same way we are.

The word "many" is included in Proverbs 11:14 on purpose. One friend might offer some advice that you question or might not have all the wisdom you need. Sometimes additional input is required.

Proverbs offers these other reminders of the value of having friends who pursue God's wisdom:

Walk with the wise and become wise;

associate with fools and get in trouble.

(Proverbs 13:20)

Wounds from a sincere friend are

better than many kisses from an enemy.

(Proverbs 27:6)

Sometimes a wise friend might need to tell you something that hurts a little. Coming from a trustworthy person, though, that "wound" can be worth it in the long run.

Opening yourself up to counsel from wise Christian friends can be a game-changer. As we discussed earlier, faith isn't a solo sport. **So find safety—and support—in numbers, with friends who follow Jesus.**

NOW THAT I GO TO CHURCH, MY OLD FRIENDS THINK I'M WEIRD

Our culture is obsessed with what's popular, tracking every move of celebrities and creating all kinds of lists and rankings. **In a recent poll, Americans named Jesus the second most popular historical person, after Abraham Lincoln.** (I'm from Illinois, the land of Lincoln, but ahead of Jesus? Wow!)

Even if people aren't obsessed with popularity, most of them want to be liked. It feels good when lots of people accept you. But doing something that goes against the flow or stands out as different can make you feel like an outsider.

Deciding to follow Jesus might mean living a bit differently. Some of your friends might think attending church is weird, or they might criticize you for avoiding things you used to do. Those comments can sting—and even make you wonder if you made the right choice.

God built into you a desire to feel important and significant. News flash: You are! **God prizes you because he created you.** When you grasp that truth, it helps you live differently.

You won't be so concerned with what your non-Christian friends think because you know your significance comes not from the approval of friends but from God.

I love Ephesians 2:10. It says:

> For we are God's masterpiece. He has created us anew in Christ Jesus.

No matter what your friends say, you're a priceless masterpiece. **Your worth doesn't rise and fall.**

Jesus, the best friend you can ever have, values you so highly he died for you—so you can be with him forever.

WHY DO PEOPLE SOMETIMES ACT DIFFERENTLY AT CHURCH AND AT SCHOOL?

Being a Christian gives you insider information on the source of your significance and value. But holding on to that truth 100 percent of the time can be tough.

Most young people are trying to work out their identity; it's a natural part of that life stage. So kids attend church for many different reasons. Some go because they honestly want to learn more about Jesus. Some go because their parents say, "Get in the car!" Some are there because of friends. Others go to church because they think Jesus wants them to, and if they do enough "religious things," Jesus will be happy and let them into heaven.

As a follower of Jesus, you know attending church doesn't make someone a Christian. Being a Christian means realizing your sins separate you from God, and the only way to eliminate that separation is to accept Jesus' free gifts of forgiveness and new life. By entering a relationship with Jesus, you've chosen to make him your Savior and let him lead your life.

But you can't know someone else's heart or whether they really understand Christianity. They may not realize why going to church matters. Some of your peers are probably confused about their faith. When they face challenges—especially at school—they may choose what's most popular or accepted. Maybe they just aren't ready to put Jesus first in their lives.

The best thing is to pray for that person to put Jesus first all the time. **If you're really good friends with someone who acts differently at church and school, talk to them about what you're seeing, but be encouraging rather than judgmental.**

Ask questions and care. Life can be tough enough; everyone needs grace and kindness along the way.

WHY DO *I* SOMETIMES ACT DIFFERENTLY AT CHURCH AND AT SCHOOL?

After a church camp or youth retreat, you probably feel excited about what you've learned. You've been having fun with friends, and you're pumped by new insights about Jesus and your life with him.

Then the school week starts…and Jesus seems farther away. Near your locker, you overhear a good friend ripping on someone else. You know Jesus stands up for people and wants you to do the same. Yet these kids are part of the cool group, and if you don't join in, they might tease you next. Then you head to math class, and during a pop quiz, the kid next to you whispers, "What'd you get for #4?" You know Jesus isn't about cheating; he wants you to be truthful. But if you don't share the answer, you'll look like a jerk.

These types of faith challenges are normal. **Living in both the "church world" and your "real world" is tougher than some people think.** How can you handle the collision of those two selves?

The Bible offers wisdom about this. In the Old Testament, a guy named Daniel was a captive in Babylon and probably scared for his life. He wasn't in a position to stand up for his beliefs. **But Daniel loved God so much he decided to do things God's way, no matter the consequences.**

Check out what happened:

But Daniel was determined not to defile himself by eating the food and wine given to them by the king. He asked the chief of staff for permission not to eat these unacceptable foods. **(Daniel 1:8)**

After just 10 days of eating only vegetables and water, Daniel and his God-following friends were healthier than the guys who'd been eating the food assigned by the king.

Following Jesus takes determination. It means making up your mind to do things his way before tough situations arise. Remember, you aren't alone in these struggles. **Jesus walks with you, giving you his strength each day:**

Don't be afraid, for I am with you. Don't be discouraged, for I am your God. I will strengthen you and help you. I will hold you up with my victorious right hand.

Isaiah 41:10

If you're determined to live for Jesus, he promises to help you deal with challenges. Make up your mind now so you won't be swayed by people at school or anywhere else. Jesus will help you—it's a promise!

SECTION 7:

TELL

WHAT DOES EVANGELISM MEAN?

Evangelism, a church word you'll probably hear a lot, comes from a word that means "bringing good news."

Perhaps you've anxiously waited to hear whether you were accepted into a program, camp, or college. When the big day finally arrived, the person who delivered that exciting news (whether by phone, letter, email, or text) was kind of an evangelist.

Basically, evangelism involves pointing people to Jesus.
Why is that important? Life is best with Jesus at the center. Without Jesus, life is purposeless and painful.

When Jesus recruited his first disciples, he was clear he wanted them to follow him. But he was also clear about the reason. Jesus told Peter and Andrew he'd help them "become" something. Not holy and good. Not nicer than others. Not smart about God. Nope. Of all the things Jesus could've told them, he said:

"Come, follow me, and I will show you how to fish for people!" **Mark 1:17**

You want me to do *what?*

Fishing for people might sound weird to us, but it would've made sense to Jesus' first followers. These guys caught fish for a living, so Jesus was speaking their language. "Fishing for people" is how Jesus wants us to operate, too.

Each of us is capable of being an evangelist, sharing the good news of Jesus with our friends. Think right now about someone who doesn't know Jesus, or a friend who attends church but might not have a relationship with Jesus. Start a conversation by asking, "What do you think about Jesus?" "Do you ever think there's a God who created everything?" "Do you think there's a heaven?" Or work Jesus into another conversation you're having, always listening carefully to what the other person thinks.

Your friend might not want to talk about faith right then. Or they might chat for a little while and move on. Or they might be completely open to talking about Jesus. No matter the reaction, be okay with where he or she is at.

And continue being an evangelist, sharing the good news and fishing for people whenever you can.

BUT I DON'T KNOW WHAT TO SAY!

Every year on July 11 (7/11), most 7-Eleven stores give out free Slurpees. My family and I text a bunch of friends and meet for some brain-freezing goodness.

When you have fantastic news, naturally you want to share it with friends. And nothing's more fantastic than discovering Jesus. In Acts 1:8, he says:

"You will be my witnesses, telling people about me everywhere."

What an honor! To be honest, that also sounds a little intimidating. Many Christians, even those who've known Jesus a long time, have a tough time telling others about him. They might be afraid of what people will think of them if they talk about their faith. They might not know what to do if a friend has a question they can't answer. They might just be nervous or not know how to bring up the topic.

After a guy named Philip started following Jesus, one of the first things he did was go find his friend Nathanael. But instead of just telling Nathanael about Jesus, Philip invited him to "come and see for yourself" (John 1:46).

That's a great strategy to use with your friends, as well. As a new or kind-of-new Christian, maybe you don't feel ready to talk about Jesus, but you can definitely invite someone to church with you and let them start seeing faith in action.

You don't need all the answers; you just need to be willing to offer an invitation. My family and I don't know every detail about how Slurpees are made (that's probably a good thing), but we sure enjoy telling people when they're free.

So even though you're still learning about Jesus, you can share with your friends how amazing he is. They'll be grateful you did.

YOUR FRIENDS NEED JESUS, TOO

When you first met Jesus, how did you feel? Were you excited? nervous? overwhelmed? Or maybe you felt peaceful, as if a weight had been lifted off you for the first time.

Receiving Jesus as your Lord and Savior is an incredible privilege. No one deserves his free gifts of salvation and eternal life:

> For everyone has sinned; we all fall short of God's glorious standard. **Romans 3:23**

Yet because God loved us enough to send his Son Jesus to die for us, everyone who believes in him is assured of spending eternity in heaven.

Before you knew Jesus, quite likely someone was praying that you would know and follow him. Perhaps it was a parent, friend, or youth pastor—or maybe all of the above. If you get a chance, thank them for praying for you. They've been part of changing your eternity, which is quite an honor.

Now you have the honor to be part of changing someone else's eternity. Many more people like you haven't yet heard about Jesus or chosen to know him. You probably have friends in those categories, and they need the life change Jesus offers—just as you did.

Take a minute and think of one or two friends who don't yet know Jesus. **Pray for them right now, and picture how their lives will be different if they know Jesus.** Ask that Jesus will open their hearts to him and provide opportunities for them to hear about and follow him.

Keep praying for those friends regularly. Maybe someday they'll thank you for being part of their journey to a relationship with Jesus.

YOU ARE GOD'S "PLAN A"

Say you're walking down the street and suddenly need to go to the bathroom. Fortunately, you see a public toilet. The outside has a cool mirrored look, but obviously no one can see inside. And you don't care, because you really need to go. But then you open the door and realize what it's like to see everything around you…

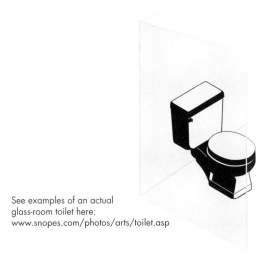

See examples of an actual glass-room toilet here: www.snopes.com/photos/arts/toilet.asp

Even with the one-way glass, it would feel pretty unnatural to go to the bathroom while you looked at all the people walking by. It's certainly not the kind of bathroom experience you'd expect. But hey, if you've gotta go, you've gotta go, right?

Here's the thing: **Faith in Jesus isn't what most people expect, either.** When they think about how to "get right" with God and end up in heaven, most people assume they need to do more good stuff than bad stuff.

Now that you're a Christian, you realize faith isn't about being good enough. Only Jesus was sinless. Faith is about understanding what Jesus did for us on the cross, but that's not what people expect.

The reason it's so important to talk to people about your faith, even if it feels scary or unnatural, is because you are God's "Plan A" for helping your friends know Jesus.

Of course, Jesus is powerful enough to make himself known any way he'd like. He could show up on your friend's doorstep or make an announcement from heaven to a classroom at school. But Jesus chooses to communicate through people just like you. Your friendships are one of the main ways you can let others know about Jesus' love and forgiveness.

Don't miss the opportunity to be part of God's plan. He wants to change your friends' lives and hopes you're ready and willing to let him work through you.

WHAT DOES IT MEAN TO BE SALT AND LIGHT?

What's your favorite pizza topping: pepperoni? veggies? Mine is BBQ chicken. The right topping sure makes pizza taste amazing.

Before you put this book down and head to the kitchen, let's talk about flavor, Bible-style. In Matthew 5:13, Jesus says:

> "You are the salt of the earth. But what good is salt if it has lost its flavor? Can you make it salty again? It will be thrown out and trampled underfoot as worthless."

In Bible times, salt was really important, not only to add flavor but also to preserve food. Salt with no flavor adds no value to food. Jesus compares Christians to salt, saying if they aren't influencing the world—adding impact and affecting what's happening—he can't use them. **Just as flavor brings out the best in your food, you can bring out the best in other people.**

Here's what Jesus says next:

"You are the light of the world—like a city on a hilltop that cannot be hidden. No one lights a lamp and then puts it under a basket. Instead, a lamp is placed on a stand, where it gives light to everyone in the house. In the same way, let your good deeds shine out for all to see, so that everyone will praise your heavenly Father." **Matthew 5:14-15**

When you live for Jesus, the light you shine makes a difference in the world. Jesus gives you the privilege and joy of bringing his light to dark places and to people who don't yet know him.

So instead of hiding your light, be willing to shine for Jesus everywhere you go. And the next time someone discusses pizza toppings, remember to be salt and light, seasoning the world for Jesus.

THE ESSENTIAL GUIDE TO

MY NEW LIFE
WITH JESUS

SECTION 8:

DOUBTS & CHALLENGES

FAITH ISN'T FAITH
WITHOUT DOUBT

Some people think having faith means never having doubts. But as my friend John Ortberg said, "As long as you have faith, you will have doubts."

Imagine I'm holding out my closed fist, and I say I'll give you the $100 bill that's inside. Would you believe me? When I open my hand and show you that I do or don't have the money, that will actually destroy your faith. Why? Because as soon as I open my fist, you'll know for sure if I have the $100 or not. Faith is no longer needed.

Faith is required only when you don't know something for sure. Many people say, "I can't be a Christian because I don't know for sure." **But when doubts are gone, you don't need faith!**

Having doubts, by contrast, doesn't mean you don't have faith. First Corinthians 13:12 says:

> Now we see things imperfectly, like puzzling reflections in a mirror, but then we will see everything with perfect clarity.

In other words, we won't understand everything until we're with Jesus in heaven.

Sometimes when you're experiencing doubt, fellow Christians might say, "You just need to have more faith." But doubt isn't necessarily a bad thing.

Jesus addressed this when one of his disciples doubted. The guy's name was Thomas, and he's even known as Doubting Thomas! When you read these verses, look closely at how Jesus reacted to Thomas' doubt. Was Jesus angry? frustrated? disappointed?

> *That Sunday evening the disciples were meeting behind locked doors because they were afraid of the Jewish leaders. Suddenly, Jesus was standing there among them! "Peace be with you," he said. As he spoke, he showed them the wounds in his hands and his side. They were filled with joy when they saw the*

Lord! Again he said, "Peace be with you. As the Father has sent me, so I am sending you." Then he breathed on them and said, "Receive the Holy Spirit. If you forgive anyone's sins, they are forgiven. If you do not forgive them, they are not forgiven."

One of the twelve disciples, Thomas (nicknamed the Twin), was not with the others when Jesus came. They told him, "We have seen the Lord!"

But he replied, "I won't believe it unless I see the nail wounds in his hands, put my fingers into them, and place my hand into the wound in his side."

Eight days later the disciples were together again, and this time Thomas was with them. The doors were locked; but suddenly, as before, Jesus was standing among them. "Peace be with you," he said. Then he said to Thomas, "Put your finger here, and look at my hands. Put your hand into the wound in my side. Don't be faithless any longer. Believe!"

"My Lord and my God!" Thomas exclaimed.

Then Jesus told him, "You believe because you have seen me. Blessed are those who believe without seeing me."

John 20:19-29

Jesus didn't show any frustration because he realized that doubt can lead to stronger faith. It isn't helpful to stuff doubt down and pretend it's not there. Don't act as if you believe things you aren't sure of or try to believe what you think you should. **Ask questions and strengthen your faith.**

Jesus is ready for all of your questions, and he's able to help you sort through any of your doubts.

?
WHEN YOU HAVE QUESTIONS

So if doubt is okay, does it matter how you express it? I think it does.

In Mark 9:14-24, the Bible describes a guy who used his doubt in a productive way:

> When they returned to the other disciples, they saw a large crowd surrounding them, and some teachers of religious law were arguing with them. When the crowd saw Jesus, they were overwhelmed with awe, and they ran to greet him.
>
> "What is all this arguing about?" Jesus asked.
>
> One of the men in the crowd spoke up and said, "Teacher, I brought my son so you could heal him. He is possessed by an evil spirit that won't let him talk. And whenever this spirit seizes him, it throws him violently to the ground. Then he foams at the mouth and grinds his teeth and becomes rigid. So I asked your disciples to cast out the evil spirit, but they couldn't do it."

Jesus said to them, "You faithless people! How long must I be with you? How long must I put up with you? Bring the boy to me."

So they brought the boy. But when the evil spirit saw Jesus, it threw the child into a violent convulsion, and he fell to the ground, writhing and foaming at the mouth.

"How long has this been happening?" Jesus asked the boy's father.

He replied, "Since he was a little boy. The spirit often throws him into the fire or into water, trying to kill him. Have mercy on us and help us, if you can."

"What do you mean, 'If I can'?" Jesus asked. "Anything is possible if a person believes."

The father instantly cried out, "I do believe, but help me overcome my unbelief!"

I love that last line. "Help me overcome my unbelief." Does it sound like that father had any doubts? Definitely! When I first read that, I thought, "Come on, dude. Do you believe or don't you? You can't do both…right?"

We already mentioned that as long as you have faith, you'll have doubts. But you can deal with those doubts in two different ways:

1. Cross-my-arms doubt.

This kind of doubt says, "I've pretty much decided, and I just don't believe it." If I told you I'd magically appear in your kitchen in 30 seconds, I'm not sure you'd believe me. (Actually, I hope you wouldn't!) This kind of doubt says, "Nope, not true. End of discussion." When it comes to faith, this kind of doubt isn't helpful.

2. Lift-my-eyes doubt.

Sometimes when I talk to Jesus, I look up to the sky—not because I think I'll see Jesus in the clouds but because it helps me think about looking to him for help. Lift-my-eyes doubt says, "Jesus, I want to believe. Show me how it can be possible. I'm looking and trusting." This kind of doubt is open to Jesus and has faith that he can help you figure it out.

You *will* have doubts, but don't cross your arms and quit. Instead, lift your eyes and ask Jesus for more insights. And don't be afraid to talk about your doubts with other Christians. You aren't alone in your questions.

Chances are, if you've wondered something, another person probably has, too.

WHAT ABOUT OTHER RELIGIONS?

This is a big question, and I don't want to oversimplify it. People write whole books about the topic, and it's worth a longer conversation with a Christian you trust.

But let's look at a fascinating episode in the Bible (in John 3) about a guy named Nicodemus. He was a Jewish religious leader called a Pharisee, so he didn't follow Jesus. Pharisees were experts on the many Jewish laws and took them very seriously. In fact, Pharisees believed following religious rules was the only way to get right with God.

(Go grab your Bible right now and read John chapter 3. It's short but important. I'll wait!)

During Jesus' day, regulations existed about what you could eat, what you could wear, who you could hang out with, how you were supposed to worship—everything you can imagine. How well people followed these rules supposedly showed how devoted they were to God. **But none of the rules could change someone's heart.** A Pharisee could be the best rule-follower ever yet still be a jerk and not care about anyone else.

Deep inside, Nicodemus struggled with this. Because no one can follow the law perfectly, he secretly wondered how much law-following was good enough to earn God's love. Nicodemus also saw that Jesus was more interested in people and their hearts than in laws and rules. It was very confusing, because Nicodemus cared about rules but wanted to be right with God.

Nicodemus' religion was like trying to climb a ladder to be nearer to God. All kinds of things—from saying the right kind of prayer to washing your hands the right way—could move you up the ladder. But Jesus cared more about loving people. So when Nicodemus started asking questions about religion, Jesus essentially said—in a nice way—"You've got it all backwards."

Every religion besides Christianity is about following the rules. Different religions describe what behavior is good enough to earn favor with their particular god. Sometimes those things are positive, such as being kind or serving others. But the focus is all on what a person needs to do.

Christianity, by contrast, is only about what Jesus has already done.

You can't do anything to earn God's favor. It's not about how much you go to church or how you behave. Instead, salvation is a free gift you just accept.

Following Jesus is about relationship, not rules. His death, done out of love for us, was full payment for the sins of all people.

Believing in and following Jesus is the only way to spend eternity with him. (If you didn't read John chapter 3 earlier, do it now!)

BREAKING BAD HABITS

Does anyone in your family have a bad habit? Maybe your brother chews his fingernails or your mom snores so loudly you can hear it through the wall. A bad habit can be a small thing, but it also can be more serious, affecting your health or your future.

Because humans sin, we all have bad habits. Be assured, though, that Jesus isn't impatiently tapping his finger, demanding you change everything overnight. He cares about your heart becoming more like his. **So as you get to know Jesus better, you'll begin to notice habits you want to change.**

The Bible talks about a significant habit that can be a danger for new and veteran Christians: idolatry. That isn't just about worshipping statues.

Idolatry is when you make something so important in your life that it takes Jesus' rightful place or blocks your connection to him.

When you were younger, your life might have been dominated by a certain toy, TV show, or superhero. You loved it, maybe more than anything. It was like an idol.

These days, maybe sports, technology, achievements, fashion, friends, or relaxing plays a major role in your life. Those things aren't necessarily bad, but if you make any of them a top priority above Jesus, that's idolatry.

Jesus desires the central place in your life because he wants to help you live best, and he knows that nothing else can fulfill you the way he does. Life really is better with Jesus at the center.

How can you break any bad habit of letting your possessions, activities, or friends become more important than Jesus? He can help you—daily.

In math class, you've probably seen this symbol, which means "less than":

Recently I wrote < Jesus on a sticker and placed it on my phone. It reminds me that my time spent on technology is less important than the time I spend with Jesus.

Consider putting < Jesus somewhere to remind you to make Jesus your first priority. It's a powerful way to establish good, new habits that will impact the rest of your life.

STANDING UP TO TEMPTATION

So you're getting into the rhythm of following Jesus and trying to live out his love. Then boom! Out of nowhere, temptation blindsides you. It might involve gossiping, pursuing popularity, or using drugs, alcohol, or pornography. I don't know what your temptation might be, but giving in to it moves you in the opposite direction from Jesus.

Jesus isn't surprised by the temptations you face; he faced them, too. But Jesus fought off every single one. Check out Matthew 4:1-11, which describes Jesus being tempted by Satan. Jesus was prepared to beat temptation because he knew Scripture so well he could fight off the enemy's lies with God's truth.

The kind of lies you face will sound different from the ones Jesus heard. Your temptations might sound like "It's no big deal" or "Don't worry about it—no one will ever know" or "Just one time won't hurt anybody." But giving in even a little makes saying "yes" the next time easier. And before you know it, you're out of sync with Jesus and feeling rotten.

Jesus is so good he put a plan in place so you aren't alone in moments of temptation. First Corinthians 10:13 says:

> The temptations in your life are no different from what others experience. And God is faithful. He will not allow the temptation to be more than you can stand. When you are tempted, he will show you a way out so that you can endure.

Not only does Jesus understand your battles, he also provides a special weapon. The Holy Spirit helps you stand strong against temptation and find a way out…if you're willing to listen to him. (To learn more about the Holy Spirit, turn to page 128.)

The best way to defend yourself against temptation is to be ready to fight it. Here's how:

If hanging out with a group of friends usually ends up in temptation, look for new friends. If you know a particular place causes temptation, figure out a way to steer clear.

If you know some friends will be surfing a website you don't want to see, know what you'll say or do beforehand. Or memorize a Bible verse to say to yourself, such as Philippians 4:13 (look it up!).

Ask a wise friend to help you be smart. You need to be willing to share what's tempting so your coach knows how to encourage you. Don't miss the chance to experience this kind of friendship and accountability.

Ask Jesus to help you choose his way. When you do mess up, remember that Jesus is forgiving. He's ready to offer a fresh start—and his continued strength to fight off temptation—whenever you need it.

THE ESSENTIAL GUIDE TO

MY NEW LIFE
WITH JESUS

SECTION 9:

ANSWERS TO SOME CHURCHY QUESTIONS

WHAT IS WORSHIP, AND WHY IS IT IMPORTANT?

"Worship" is a word that makes more sense when you know its origin. It comes from the old English "worthship," which means to announce the value of something or declare that it's worth a lot.

Think about how people use "worship" for things that have nothing to do with Jesus. "Their donuts are so good; I worship that place." Or "He likes that girl so much, he worships the ground she walks on." Those are value statements, though it's weird to worship the ground.

Worship often gets attached to the part of a church service when singing occurs. In fact, many churches call that "worship time," when they sing worship songs. But if worship is limited to that slot, we're really missing out.

You announce Jesus' value not just by your voice but with your actions.

Every time you do something that Jesus would do, you're actually worshipping him. When you go out of your way to help someone, that's worship. When you speak encouraging words to someone, that's worship. When you resolve a difficult situation in a way that honors Jesus…yep, that's worship.

Singing worship songs is great, but you can worship Jesus with your life by what you do. And that pleases him as much as any tune.

WHAT IS BAPTISM?

A wedding ring—whether it has a huge diamond or is a simple gold band—is worn for a symbolic reason: to show that someone is married. The ring itself doesn't make you married. If I take off my ring, for example, it doesn't mean I'm suddenly "unmarried" to my wife.

Baptism is a lot like a wedding ring. It's a way of publicly showing you've chosen to follow Jesus. John the Baptist, a cousin of Jesus, taught that "people should be baptized to show that they had repented of their sins and turned to God to be forgiven" (Mark 1:4).

A baptism can be done in several different ways but always involves water. Some churches baptize people by dunking them in a tank or lake. Others sprinkle some water on a person's forehead. Some churches baptize babies, while others wait until people are older.

No matter how or when baptism happens, the water represents the death and burial of the person's sinful past. Because Jesus has washed the person clean, he or she has new life in Christ. That makes baptism a fantastic celebration!

The Bible encourages new believers to be baptized as soon as they decide to follow Jesus. If you haven't been baptized yet, talk about it with a Christian you know. Baptism is an amazing opportunity to share the news of your faith with other people.

If you're a huge fan of a sports team, it would feel strange to keep that loyalty a secret. Don't let anything get in the way of showing your loyalty to Jesus—and your joy from being his follower.

Here are three important thoughts about baptism:

1. Being baptized doesn't make you a Christian.

That happens when you admit you've sinned, accept Jesus as the only way to get right with God, and commit to follow him faithfully.

2. Baptism doesn't mean you won't sin anymore.

You're human, so you'll mess up. But Jesus will always forgive you!

You don't need to wait to be baptized until your life is "all cleaned up."

Jesus is crazy about you right now. He wants you to celebrate his love and show that you understand it.

Jesus is ready to offer you new life with him, so prepare to get wet!

WHAT IS COMMUNION?

The human brain has an incredible capacity for memory, yet everybody forgets stuff. Have you ever been well-prepared for a test, only to have the material evaporate from your brain as soon as the test lands on your desk? Or maybe a parent asks you to do something, and you really mean to do it. But later you hear a loud, angry voice and realize you forgot.

Jesus knew we'd forget things—even important things. **He knew we'd sometimes forget him and what he did for us, so he provided a cool reminder called communion.** The first communion happened the night before Jesus was put to death on the cross, when he was having his last meal with his disciples. Jesus gave them—and us—a personal way to remember him:

> As they were eating, Jesus took some bread and blessed it. Then he broke it in pieces and gave it to the disciples, saying, "Take it, for this is my body."

> And he took a cup of wine and gave thanks to God for it. He gave it to them, and they all drank from it. And he said to them, "This is my blood, which confirms the covenant between God and his people. It is poured out as a sacrifice for many." **Mark 14:22-24**

Communion isn't magic. The bread represents Jesus' body. When you eat it, Jesus wants you to remember how his body was broken because he loves you and sets you free. The drink represents Jesus' blood. That might sound strange, but it's not like a vampire movie. When you drink communion, Jesus wants you to remember he was willing to bleed and die for you. He's saying, "My pain was worth it, for you."

Churches celebrate Jesus' gift of communion in different ways. Some use certain kinds of bread or drink, and some offer communion more frequently than others. Jesus isn't concerned about how communion happens; he just wants it to happen. He gave his followers a fantastic way to remember how highly he values them.

Luke 22:19 records a key sentence Jesus said as he was giving communion to his disciples:

"Do this to remember me."

When you feel forgotten, Jesus wants you to remember he cares about you. When you don't feel good enough, Jesus wants you to remember he died for you. When you do something wrong, Jesus wants you to remember he forgives you.

> Communion is a reminder of Jesus' amazing love in action, shown for us all.

WHO IS THE HOLY SPIRIT?

When I was younger, going to church seemed rather boring—until I finally understood about the Holy Spirit. That changed my view of God, and it can change yours, too. I promise I'm not exaggerating!

First, though, it helps to know about the Trinity. That concept, which comes from a word meaning "three," says that our one true God expresses himself in three distinct persons:

GOD THE FATHER

He created us and sent Jesus, his Son, to earth to save us.

GOD THE SON

Jesus was born as a baby, later died on the cross, and then rose from the dead.

GOD THE HOLY SPIRIT

This third part of the Trinity can be tough to understand. Some churches call him the Holy Ghost, which confused me when I was younger. I thought of this:

But the Holy Spirit doesn't have anything to do with Halloween. He's an incredible gift.

Before Jesus was crucified, his disciples were worried and scared. They didn't want Jesus to die and leave them alone. But Jesus told them:

"I will ask the Father, and he will give you another Advocate, who will never leave you. He is the Holy Spirit, who leads into all truth. The world cannot receive him, because it isn't looking for him and doesn't recognize him. But you know him, because he lives with you now and later will be in you."

John 14:16-17

Jesus assured his fearful disciples they'd never be alone. **The Holy Spirit would be their guide, support, and friend.**

Have you ever felt really alone? Maybe you've worried about stuff late at night or felt misunderstood at school. **No matter what you're going through, the Holy Spirit is a guide and counselor.** Because he's God, he's good, kind, and wise. And the Holy Spirit is available to all people who follow Jesus, just as he was to the first disciples. With the Holy Spirit, you'll never be alone.

The Holy Spirit won't overpower you to get your attention, though. You need to choose to listen to him. The television in your house might be on even when no one's watching. In the same way, the Holy Spirit is always "on"—he's always with you—but you decide if you want to pay attention and listen for his direction.

Sometimes the Holy Spirit may want to tell you something, such as an encouragement or a reminder that he loves and values you. Other times, the Holy Spirit may urge you to do something, such as read your Bible regularly, say "I'm sorry" to someone, reach out to a person who needs a friend, etc.

The Holy Spirit won't prompt you to do something that's not biblical. So if you're wondering if the Holy Spirit is really leading you toward a particular action, ask yourself two questions:

Should you lie to your mom? Nope, not biblical. Paint graffiti on a building? Nope, illegal. The Holy Spirit definitely wouldn't direct you to do those things.

Jump off a three-story building? Crazy. Smile at a lonely kid at school? Sounds pretty wise, as if the Holy Spirit could be leading you to do it. If you're still not sure about a decision, ask another Christian if he or she thinks it seems biblical and wise.

When you choose to tune into the Holy Spirit's direction, your life will never be boring.

Jesus has a great adventure planned for you, and the Holy Spirit wants to guide you to and through it.

So open your ears, and see what he has in store!

THE ESSENTIAL GUIDE TO

MY NEW LIFE WITH JESUS

FINAL WORDS

I'll end this book the same way I started it—by saying congratulations! If you've read this far, it means you've invested a bunch of time thinking about your new life with Jesus. And that's one of the most awesome things I can imagine.

When I first started following Jesus, I thought having faith was like going on a road trip. I pictured Jesus leading me to Good Christian Land. (That's not a real place, but you probably know what I mean.)

Somewhere along the way, I realized that following Jesus was more about the journey than the destination.

Yes, being a Christian means you'll end up in a really great place someday—heaven. But during your journey on earth, you have the privilege of developing a relationship with Jesus, your Savior and friend.

Jesus promises to be with you the entire way, helping you deal with new situations and face new challenges. Whether you're hitting a detour or seeing jaw-dropping sites, you'll never be alone.

So get ready for the next step of your exciting journey, and keep looking to Jesus, your trustworthy travel partner.

I'm rooting for you!

—Scott